Cultures

Program Authors

Connie Juel, Ph.D.

Jeanne R. Paratore, Ed.D.

Deborah Simmons, Ph.D.

Sharon Vaughn, Ph.D.

Glenview, Illinois
Boston, Massachusetts
Chandler, Arizona
Upper Saddle River, New Jersey

ISBN-13: 978-0-328-45284-2
ISBN-10: 0-328-45284-X

8 9 10 V011 14 13
CC1

Cultures

How are communities and families similar around the world?

Dressing Up

Dressing Up

Let's Explore

Choose an activity to explore this week's concept—Dressing Up.

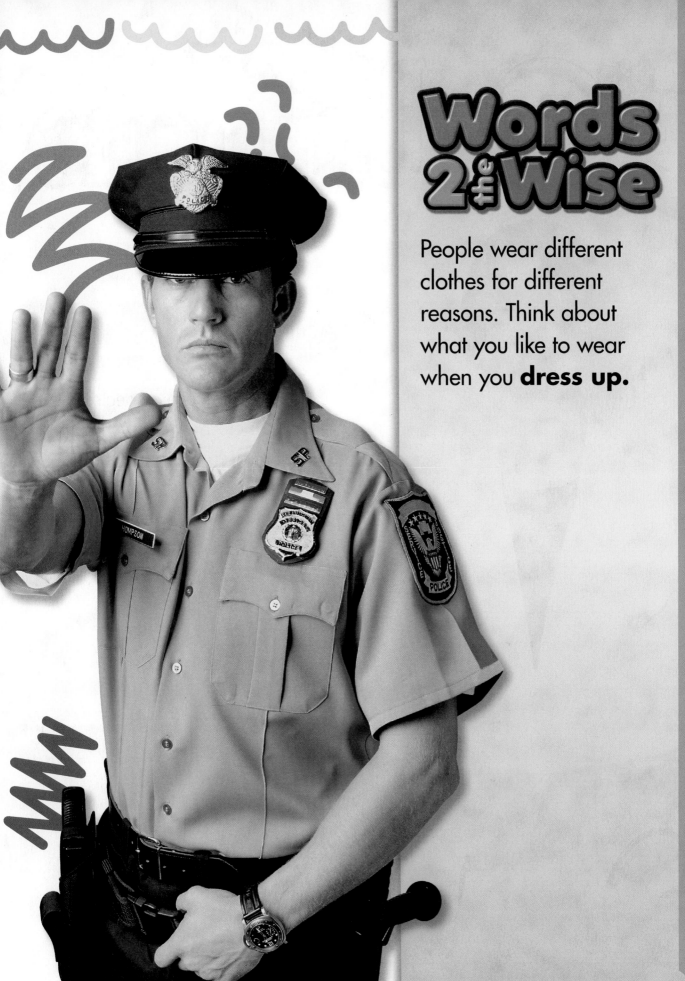

Words 2 the Wise

People wear different clothes for different reasons. Think about what you like to wear when you **dress up.**

Let's Explore Uniforms

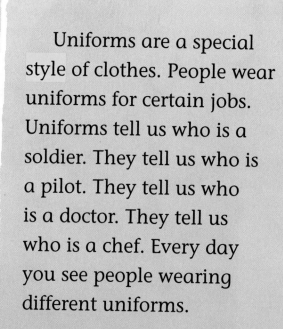

Uniforms are a special style of clothes. People wear uniforms for certain jobs. Uniforms tell us who is a soldier. They tell us who is a pilot. They tell us who is a doctor. They tell us who is a chef. Every day you see people wearing different uniforms.

People wear uniforms to help them do their jobs or so other people know what their jobs are.

The style of some uniforms has not changed. The colors have also not changed. Doctors wear white coats. Judges wear black robes in court.

Some uniforms protect workers. Firefighters wear heavy coats. They also wear helmets.

Police officers wear uniforms so people know whom to ask for help in an emergency.

Why do police wear blue clothes? London was the first city with police officers. London police wore blue coats. Now it is a tradition. Police officers in many cities wear blue. Most police officers wear the same blue clothing. They wear it every time they work.

People wear different uniforms for work and for play. Some nurses wear colorful uniforms. They have matching tops and bottoms. They call this uniform "scrubs."

People on a basketball team wear shorts and a shirt with a number on the back.

What uniforms do you wear for school, for play, or for other activities?

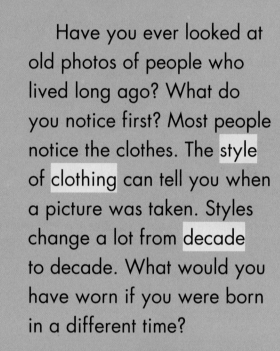

Have you ever looked at old photos of people who lived long ago? What do you notice first? Most people notice the clothes. The style of clothing can tell you when a picture was taken. Styles change a lot from decade to decade. What would you have worn if you were born in a different time?

They Wore That?

by Dennis Fertig

12

For a long time, kids wore the same style of clothes as adults. It was the custom. The clothing was stiff and tight. Kids started wearing clothes made just for them around 1850.

Clothes were made by hand in the early 1900s. Boys wore short, heavy pants. Girls weren't allowed to wear pants. Girls wore long, heavy dresses. Boys and girls wore thick stockings.

But clothing styles changed because of important world events.

The 1920s

Kids' clothing changed after World War I. Boys still wore short pants. They also wore pants that came to their knees called "knickers." Girls still wore dresses. But the dresses weren't as heavy. They also weren't as long.

The 1930s

The Great Depression began in the 1930s. People didn't have much money. They didn't have money to buy new clothes. Many kids wore clothes that were handed down. Parents sewed patches over holes.

The 1940s and 1950s

Clothing styles changed again after World War II. Many men were overseas in the 1940s. They were fighting in a war. Women worked in factories. The custom for women to only wear dresses or skirts ended. Now working women also wore pants. They wanted to be more comfortable.

Many girls wore pants by the 1950s. But they wore them only at home. Boys and girls still dressed up for school. They still dressed up to go places.

The 1960s

Clothing styles changed again in the 1960s. Boys and girls still dressed up for school. But at home clothes became more colorful and fun. Girls wore pants or short skirts. Boys wore jeans and tie-dyed shirts. These shirts were dyed all different colors.

Bell-Bottoms and Hip-Huggers

Bell-bottoms and hip-huggers were two styles of pants that were very popular in the 1960s. Bell-bottoms were wide around the feet. They reminded people of bells. They were originally designed for sailors in the Navy. Hip-huggers also had bell-bottoms. Hip-huggers only went up to the hip. Most pants were worn at the waist.

The 1970s

Children still wore colorful clothes in the 1970s. They started wearing jeans and T-shirts to school in this decade. They weren't expected to dress up as much. T-shirts with funny sayings or pictures were popular.

The 1980s

Clothing styles changed very quickly in the 1980s. TV changed how kids dressed. Kids wanted to wear clothes they saw on TV. They had plenty of styles to choose from. Sports such as basketball were popular. Boys wore shorts and long socks to play basketball.

The 1990s

Kids watched commercials on TV in the 1990s. They saw ads for clothes. Brand-name clothes became popular. Some kids wore designer shirts, pants, and shoes. The name of the designer was shown on the outside. Many brands were expensive.

Brand-name means something made by a well-known person or company.

I Saw It on TV

Most families had at least one TV at home by the 1980s. Kids wore T-shirts with their favorite cartoon characters on them. They bought clothes that TV stars wore.

What Do YOU Think?

How are clothes kids wore in the 1900s different from the clothes you wear today? How are they the same?

INTERNATIONAL Day

by Amy Cruz
illustrated by David Sheldon

**Fay Lee was nervous.
Today was not an ordinary day.**

The principal's name was
Ms. Menacho. Ms. Menacho
had asked Fay to take photos for
International Day. She wanted
some good pictures for the
school newspaper. *So why did
Ms. Menacho ask me to take
pictures?* Fay asked herself.
Fay had never taken pictures
before. She was worried her
pictures would be ordinary.

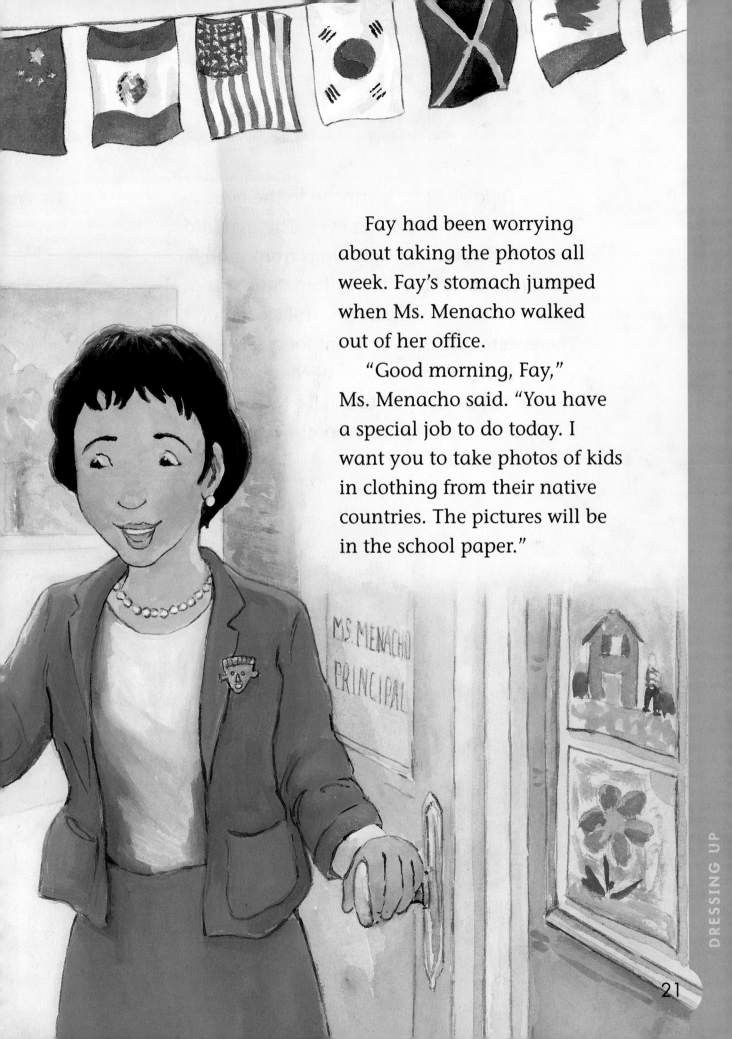

Fay had been worrying about taking the photos all week. Fay's stomach jumped when Ms. Menacho walked out of her office.

"Good morning, Fay," Ms. Menacho said. "You have a special job to do today. I want you to take photos of kids in clothing from their native countries. The pictures will be in the school paper."

MS MENACHO
PRINCIPAL

Fay followed Ms. Menacho to the gym.
Fay could not believe her eyes. The gym did
not look the same. Bright flags from many
countries hung from the ceiling. Students and
teachers were dressed in colorful clothing.
There were tables of different foods.

Fay pointed the camera at Ms. Menacho.
The principal stopped to talk to Michael and
Ella. The twins stood in a booth that read,
"Ghana, Africa."

Fay looked at Tommy through the camera. All she could see were his bright red clothes. They were from his native country of China. Tommy showed Ms. Menacho a jade dragon. She really liked it.

Ms. Menacho visited one booth after another. She talked to students. She tried traditional foods. Fay took picture after picture. She hoped the photos turned out nicely.

Soon the celebration was over. Fay followed Ms. Menacho back to her office.

Fay sat at a computer. She studied the photos she had taken. She was surprised at how nice the pictures looked. Fay was proud of her work.

Fay looked at a picture of Tommy. He was smiling widely in his red costume. She zoomed in on the small jade dragon he was holding.

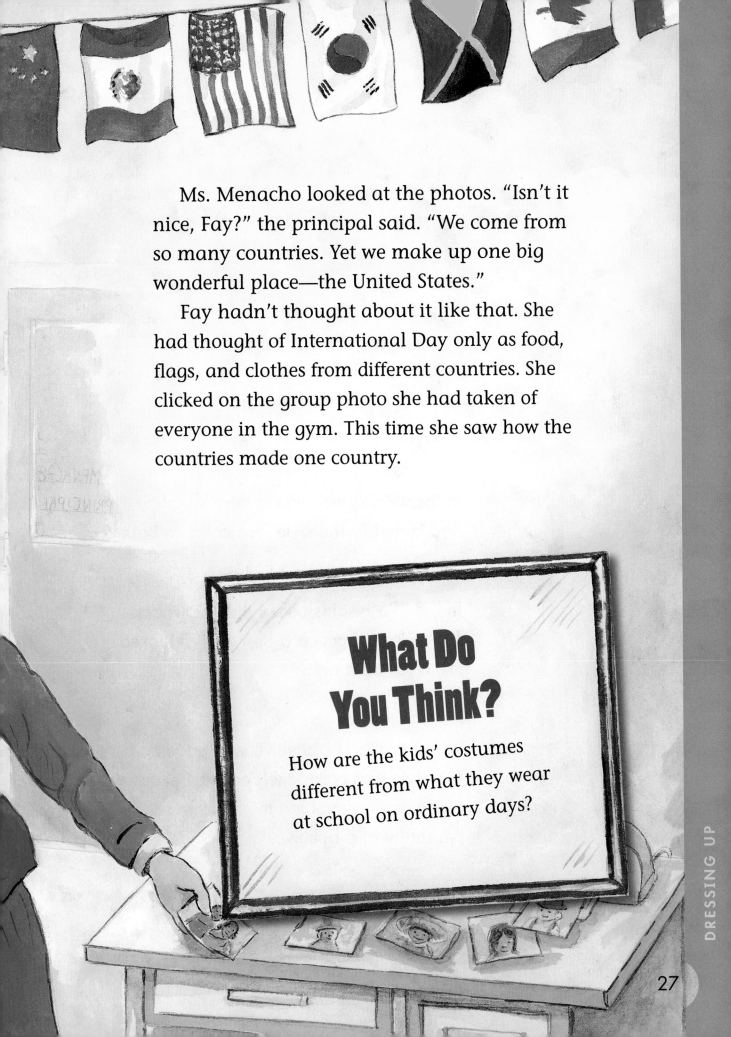

Ms. Menacho looked at the photos. "Isn't it nice, Fay?" the principal said. "We come from so many countries. Yet we make up one big wonderful place—the United States."

Fay hadn't thought about it like that. She had thought of International Day only as food, flags, and clothes from different countries. She clicked on the group photo she had taken of everyone in the gym. This time she saw how the countries made one country.

What Do You Think?

How are the kids' costumes different from what they wear at school on ordinary days?

Hair-Raising Styles!

Paying attention to hair is not new. Let's look at styles from the past.

Bobbed and Beautiful

In the 1920s, women cut their long hair and curled it. The style was called a bob.

The Pony Tail

In the 1950s, girls pulled their hair back. The style was called a pony tail. It looked like a tail on a pony.

The Bigger the Better

In the 1960s, the beehive was popular. The style was called the beehive because hair was piled high on the head into the shape of a beehive!

What does your hair say about YOU?

The Rachel

In the 1990s, Jennifer Aniston's hairstyle on the TV show *Friends* was copied by thousands of women. The style was called "The Rachel," after the character's name on the show.

Wigs, Crew Cuts, Mohawks

Men's hairstyles have changed too. Hundreds of years ago, men wore long wigs. Since the 1930s, a very short hairstyle called a crew cut has been popular. In the 1960s, some men grew long hair. In the 1980s, a style called the mohawk was popular.

4 you 2 Do

Word Play

Sometimes styles change a little and sometimes they change in a big way. Words can be like that too. Change the vocabulary words below so that they are spelled differently. Use the endings -s or -es, -al, or al + ly.

tradition   clothing

Making Connections

Fay's school had a special day when kids would dress up in traditional costumes. Pretend your school has a Decade Day. What decade's clothing would you choose to wear? What would your choice of clothing tell about you?

On Paper

Different events changed clothing styles from decade to decade. Think about International Day at Fay's school. Why don't kids wear clothing from their native countries every day?

Our World

Contents

Our World

Words 2 the Wise

People from around **Our World** are alike in many ways. As you read think about things that we all share.

Let's Explore

TOWN SQUARES

Fountain in town square, Seville, Spain

A town square forms the heart of many towns. It is an open area. It has buildings on all sides. A town square is a place for people to enjoy parties. They enjoy dances there. They enjoy feasts and holidays. There are town squares all over the world. In every country these are public places that everyone knows. They are always crawling with life!

Temples, statues, and people in a square in Patan, Nepal

Market Square, Warsaw, Poland

ACROSS THE OCEAN

by Alef Lett

Japan and America are separated by the Pacific Ocean. But ideas travel between these countries. Japan often picks up clothing styles from America. It also picks up foods. It picks up entertainment. Some English words have become part of the Japanese language. Many Japanese things are popular in America too.

Japanese and American people like similar things. Let's take a look at some things they share in common.

The word *karaoke* comes from the Japanese language. It means "empty band." Music plays, and people sing along.

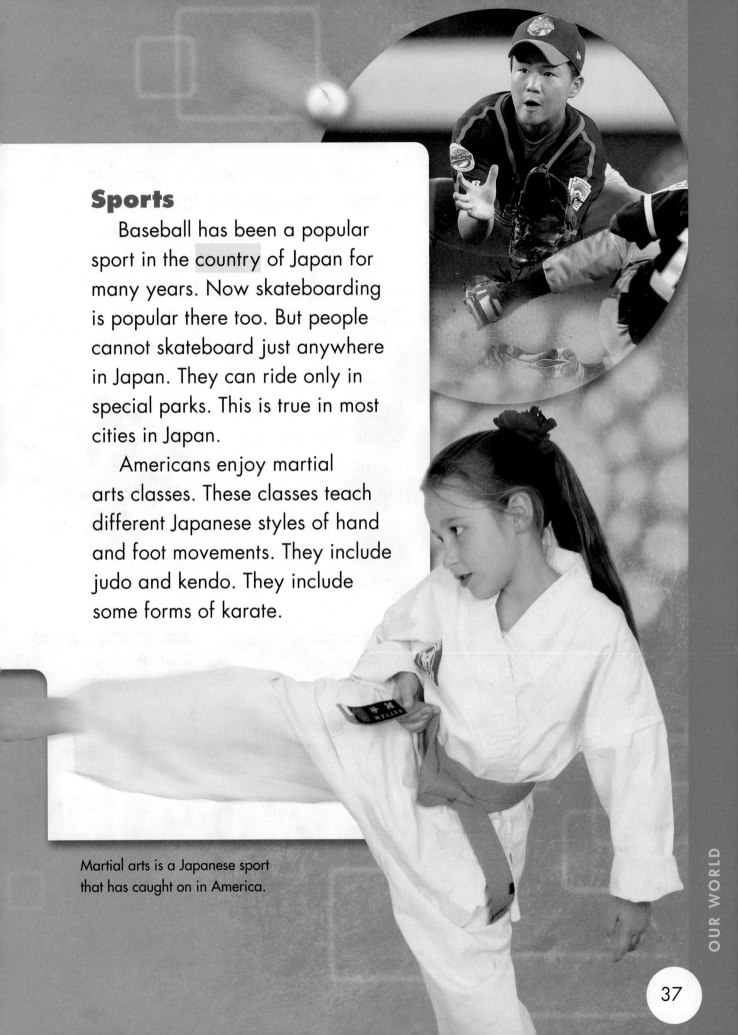

Sports

Baseball has been a popular sport in the country of Japan for many years. Now skateboarding is popular there too. But people cannot skateboard just anywhere in Japan. They can ride only in special parks. This is true in most cities in Japan.

Americans enjoy martial arts classes. These classes teach different Japanese styles of hand and foot movements. They include judo and kendo. They include some forms of karate.

Martial arts is a Japanese sport that has caught on in America.

Food

American fast foods are popular in Japan. You can find fast-food restaurants in most Japanese cities.

At first Japanese farmers worried about fast food in Japan. They were afraid people would stop eating rice. Rice is a main food in Japan. The farmers began promoting rice bread. People love the new bread. But there is no need to worry. People in Japan still eat plenty of rice and rice dishes.

American travelers can find fast food everywhere in Japan.

Food ideas have also traveled from Japan to America. Sushi is one type of Japanese food that many Americans enjoy. It may be made with rice and vegetables. It may be made with pickles, eggs, or raw fish. They are arranged in layers. Then they are wrapped in seaweed. They are cut into small rolls. Americans also like to eat rice. They like to eat noodle dishes.

This girl uses chopsticks to eat her noodles. The Japanese use them instead of forks and knives.

People in Japan give chocolates for Valentine's Day just like we do.

Holidays

Chocolate is a big part of Valentine's Day in America. Did you know that's true in Japan too? There's one big difference. The girls and women in Japan give chocolate to boys and men.

However, Japanese men give women and girls chocolates on March 14. This holiday is called White Day. White marshmallows were originally the gifts that were given. Then people gave chocolates.

Entertainment

Have you heard of Godzilla? This movie monster scared people in America for years. But did you know that the first Godzilla movie was made in Japan? In Japan, the monster's name was Gojira. The monster's name was changed to Godzilla for the American movies.

Japanese comic books are also popular in America.

Some say the idea for Gojira came from an American story about a creature that lives in the sea. It lives in modern times. The creature goes to a lighthouse every time a foghorn blows.

Today many American bookstores sell Japanese comic books. Cartoons based on these comics play on TV. A character called Astro Boy has become popular in the U.S. He is a robot with human emotions. The Robot Hall of Fame even has a display about him.

Japan and America are similar in many ways. What ideas will Japan and America exchange next? Who knows? But they are sure to make life more interesting in both places!

WHAT DO YOU THINK?

What idea or thing from Japan do you like most?

Pictures

by Uma Krishnaswami
Illustrated by Gary Phillips

I had just hung up the phone with my friend Kayla. That is when my parents broke the news. "Anna, I got a job transfer. We're moving to India for a year," Dad said.

"We'll be working at an eye clinic," Mom said. "We found a school for you."

I could not believe it. I did not want to move to a different country.

I thought Kayla would be mad, but she was excited. She made me promise that I would send her a picture of an elephant.

Three months later we transferred to a place called Jaipur (JY-per). I saw many pink buildings and plenty of traffic, but no elephants. I didn't know if there were any pictures worth taking.

My school was in a pink building too. My first day was awful. I was taller than all the other kids, and no one else looked like me. I never felt so different.

The teacher's name was Mrs. Rana. She wore a colorful, cotton wrap. She called it a sari. She started with Hindi language class. I was lost!

After school I went to a tailor to get fitted for a school uniform. How would I ever learn this new culture?

"How was school?" Mom asked at dinner.

"I understand only every third word," I said. "And the accent is hard to copy. I think I need a translator."

"It can't be that bad. It's only your first day," said Mom. "Dad and I are taking Hindi language classes too."

"You'll learn the language and the culture," Dad said. "You just need to see things differently."

"See things differently?" I said.

"Be happy to see and do something new," Dad said.

In Hindi class I learned to write my name. Everyone else knew more than I did. I thought kids would make fun of me. But they didn't!

"Can I write my best friend's name?" I asked.

"Sure," said Mrs. Rana. "What is it?"

"Kayla," I said. A boy named Naru laughed.

"What's so funny?" I asked.

"That name!" said Naru. "In *our* language, Kela means *banana.*" Everyone laughed.

A week went by. I saw a camel.

"Wow, Kayla would love to see that," I said. I took a picture. India was getting more interesting everyday.

School was getting better. We made colorful cards. "Holi Hai!" said Mrs. Rana. "That means *It's Holi!* Tomorrow is a holiday."

"What is Holi?" I asked.

"We wear white clothes and throw color on everyone," said Kavita. "Come to my house. Bring your parents. We will play Holi together."

The next day, Mom, Dad, and I went to Kavita's house.
We all wore new white clothes.

Kavita's mom met us at the door. She put streaks of
color on our faces. Inside we all played Holi. We threw
colored powder and water on each other. We looked like
walking rainbows! We ate sticky sweets. We danced in a
circle. I took many pictures.

When we got back to our house, Kayla called. "I missed you at art camp," she said.

I said, "Holi Hai!" I told her what it meant.

"I have pictures to send you," I said. I thought of the many pictures I had taken in India. I was excited to send them to Kayla. Maybe seeing different things will make her happy.

What Do You Think?

Do you think Anna changed her mind about living in a different country? Why?

One Moment All Around the World

People all over the world live in different time zones. This means that at any one moment, it is a different time of day in many countries!

Berlin, Germany
4:00 PM

Hong Kong, China
11:00 PM

Denver, United States of America • 8:00 AM

Buenos Aires, Argentina • 12:00 PM

Nairobi, Kenya
6:00 PM

New Delhi, India
7:30 PM

Stacey lives in Denver, in the United States. Here, it is eight o'clock in the morning. Stacey is getting on the bus to start her day at school.

12:00 PM

But in Buenos Aires, Argentina, it is already noon! Ruben is eating his favorite lunch, empanadas. It is a very popular food in his country.

empanadas • a pastry filled with chopped meat and vegetables

4:00 PM

Emma lives in Berlin, Germany. It is four o'clock in the afternoon in Berlin. Emma is having fun at the Berlin Zoo with her dad.

6:00 PM

In Nairobi, Kenya, it is six o'clock in the evening. Kibwe and his friends just won a soccer game. It is time for everyone to head home.

7:30 PM

In New Delhi, India, it is already 7:30 at night! Iksha will have to hurry if she wants to finish her homework before bed.

11:00 PM

And in Hong Kong, China, the time is eleven o'clock. Wen is already fast asleep. He is dreaming about tomorrow.

Do you know which time zone you live in?

4 you 2 Do

Word Play

Here are some important words you read this week. Test your memory. Can you unscramble them?

aJpna   ulcutre   ndIai

ilarmis   oppluar   eaugganl

Bonus Word: usihs

Clue: What popular Japanese food do Americans enjoy?

Making Connections

Think about the children you read about this week. In what ways are children around the world more alike than different?

On Paper

You read how Japanese and American people like and do similar things. Write a letter to a Japanese student about something new in American culture that you think he or she might like.

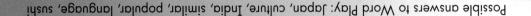

Possible answers to Word Play: Japan, culture, India, similar, popular, language, sushi

56

COMING TO AMERICA

Contents

COMING TO AMERICA

Words 2 the Wise

Many Americans originally lived in another country before **coming to America.** Think about what you know about coming to America as you read this week's selection.

Let's Explore

Coming to America

A family journeys from China to America. At first the thought of living in a new country is scary. But they are excited to learn about America. They learn to speak English. They eat American food. They wear popular clothing styles. They make new friends. But they keep many of their Chinese traditions too.

Many people in the United States teach their children that it is important to wear clothing and eat food from their native countries and from their new country.

Many **immigrants** teach their traditions to their sons and daughters. Immigrants are people who leave their country to live in another country. They also want to learn about their new country. Why is it important to keep the old while learning the new?

New York's Tenement Museum

by Robert Bland

Imagine a house with three rooms. There's one room for sitting. There's one room with a fireplace and a table. And there's one bedroom. You share a bathroom with other families. The bathroom is outside or in another hallway.

Many years ago immigrants made long journeys to America to find new jobs and a new life. These immigrants lived in buildings called tenements (TEN-uh-ments).

A tenement is a building with several floors. It has many three-room apartments. It has a bathroom everyone shares. Many families lived in one tenement building.

One of these tenements was built in 1863 in New York City. In 1988 workers turned this old tenement into a museum. The Tenement Museum tells about the families who lived there.

Many immigrant families lived in tenement buildings in New York.

The Gumpertz family ate and slept in these two rooms.

The Gumpertz (GUHM-perts) family lived in an apartment that is now part of the Tenement Museum. They moved to America from Prussia in 1874. Nathalie Gumpertz took care of four young children by herself.

Nathalie made dresses. Dresses were made by hand then. Nathalie sewed the dresses in her apartment. Women bought dresses from Nathalie. She made about eight dollars a week. Even though she was underpaid, in those days it was enough money to pay for schooling and rent.

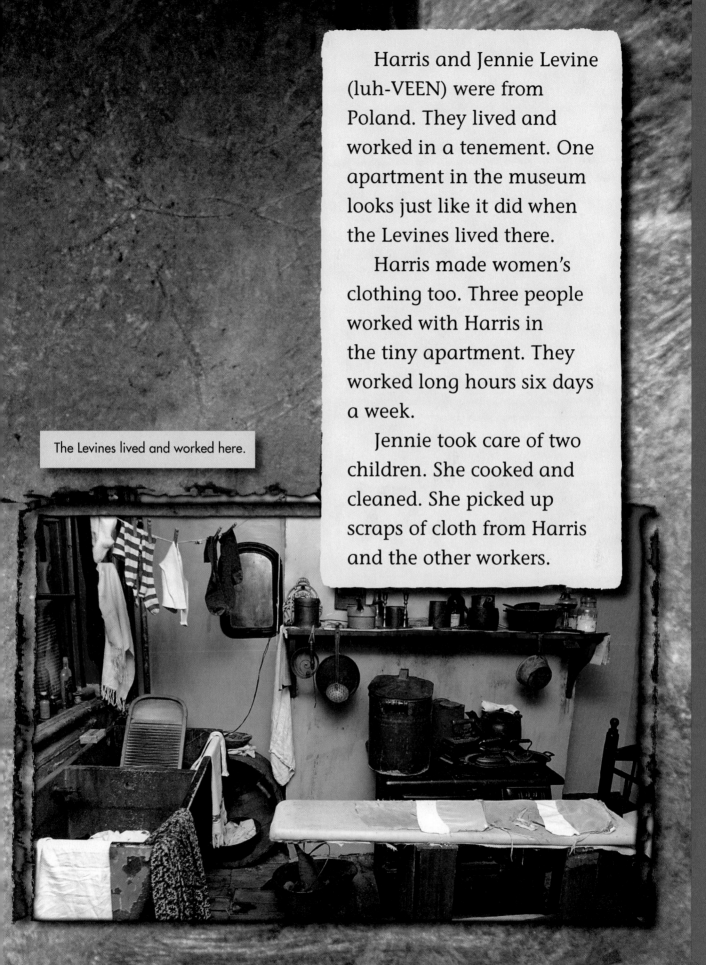

Harris and Jennie Levine (luh-VEEN) were from Poland. They lived and worked in a tenement. One apartment in the museum looks just like it did when the Levines lived there.

Harris made women's clothing too. Three people worked with Harris in the tiny apartment. They worked long hours six days a week.

Jennie took care of two children. She cooked and cleaned. She picked up scraps of cloth from Harris and the other workers.

The Levines lived and worked here.

65

The beautiful dresses were hard to make. The workers made the top part of the dress first. Then they put on the sleeves. Next, Harris and the men added the collar. Harris put the skirt on last.

A pretty dress like Harris made may have cost about ten dollars. If you go to the museum, you can see a dress that Harris might have made.

A dress like those the Levines made hangs in the front room of the museum.

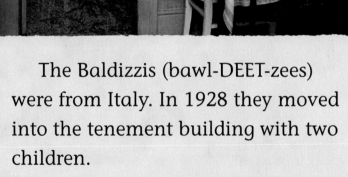

The Baldizzis lived in this apartment.

The Baldizzis (bawl-DEET-zees) were from Italy. In 1928 they moved into the tenement building with two children.

The apartment was cold and dark. The children washed each day with cold water and a cloth. They got one warm bath each week.

Mr. Baldizzi worked with wood using special tools to make money. He walked up and down streets looking for work. Sometimes he got a job. Sometimes he didn't.

Life was hard for most of the immigrants. They brought little with them. Many were very poor. They missed their old homes. Immigrants worked hard. They wanted to learn. They wanted America to be their new home.

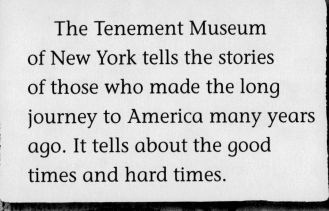

The Tenement Museum of New York tells the stories of those who made the long journey to America many years ago. It tells about the good times and hard times.

What Do You Think?

How did Harris Levine and his workers make dresses?

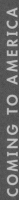

Kim Li's New Home

by Julie Lavender illustrated by Martha Aviles

Kim Li mailed her first postcard as an immigrant. That's what the people at the airport called her. Mama said that an immigrant is a person who moves from one country to another.

Dear Grandmom,
    Our journey was long. The airplane took us from Korea to America. Atlanta will be our new home. Everyone looks different here. They do not talk like me. I am glad I learned to speak English in Korea. I hope I like it here.
        Love,
        Kim Li

Kim Li was outside playing with her new friend, Jessie.

"Jessie, do you like school?" Kim Li asked.

"Yes," said Jessie. "School is fun."

Dear Grandmom,
    I met a friend today. She lives in my apartment building. Her name is Jessie. She has red hair. She moved here last year from California. Mom took a photograph of us today.
    Love,
    Kim Li

Jessie

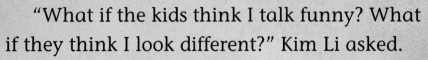

"What if the kids think I talk funny? What if they think I look different?" Kim Li asked.

Jessie said, "Oh, everyone thinks I talk funny. Where I used to live, we call our drink a *pop*. Here, it's a *soft drink*. At my old home, we say *you guys*. My friends here say *y'all*."

"But you are from America," said Kim Li.

"I know, but you don't have to be from another country to be different," Jessie said.

Dear Grandmom,
    Guess what? There is no school on Saturday. That is very different from Korea. Mom just sent you that photograph of Jessie and me. She also sent our new address.
    Love,
    Kim Li

"Hello, Kim Li," said Mrs. Alvarez. "Welcome to America. And welcome to your new school. I moved to America from Mexico when I was about your age.

I could not speak English when I first came. My friends helped me learn. Some things are the same in this country, and some things are different. I think you'll like it here."

"Everyone," said Mrs. Alvarez, "this is Kim Li. She made the long journey to America from Korea."

Mrs. Alvarez said, "Kim Li can teach us Korean words. We'll teach Kim Li how to say *y'all!*"

Later, Kim Li and her family were eating food from a restaurant down the street. "The food in America is overcooked," Mom said at dinner.

"People drive below the speed limit," Dad said.

"Please pass the carrots, y'all," Kim Li said.

Her parents laughed.

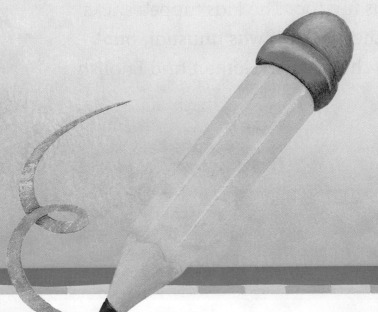

Dear Grandmom,

Today was my first day at school. I am different from the kids in my class. But they are all different too. We look different and have different addresses. Some have red hair. Some have brown hair. And some have black hair. Three kids wear glasses. One boy is very tall. We are all different, but Jessie says we are all the same.

Love,

Kim Li

Kim Li's favorite time at school was recess. The boys and girls played soccer. Kim Li played soccer in Korea.

Music was fun too. The kids tapped sticks together to the music. It was unusual, but tapping was the same in Korean and English.

Dear Grandmom,
     I miss you, and I miss Korea. But I like my new home. Things are very different here, but still they are the same. I learn new things. I teach my friends new things every day too. I hope you enjoy reading my postcards!
     Love,
     Kim Li

me

Jessie had a birthday party at her house after school. The boys and girls played soccer in the backyard. When the game was over, Jessie said, "Come inside, y'all. There's pizza and soft drinks for everyone."

What Do You Think?

What is the first event in the story that helped Kim Li learn about her new home? How did it help her?

MOVING TO

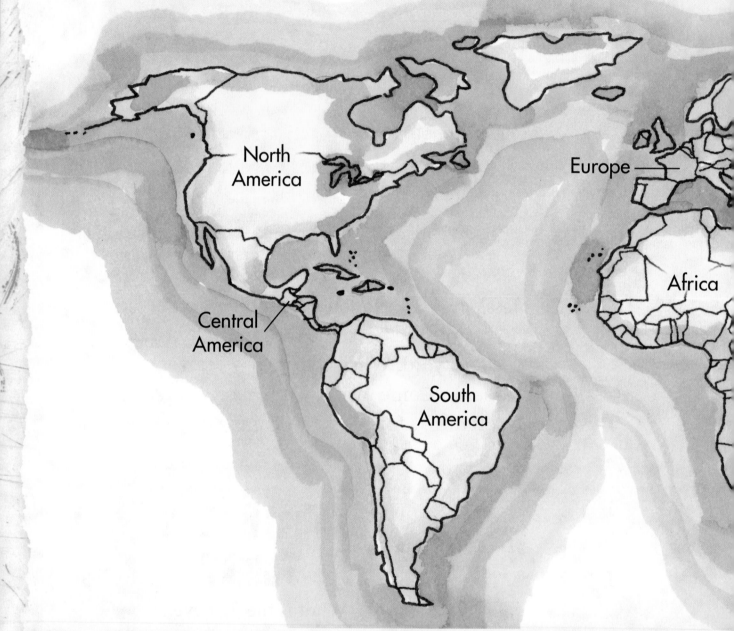

North
America

Central
America

South
America

Europe

Africa

For hundreds of years, people from all over the world have been moving to the United States. Look at the map above. Did your family come from another country?

AMERICA

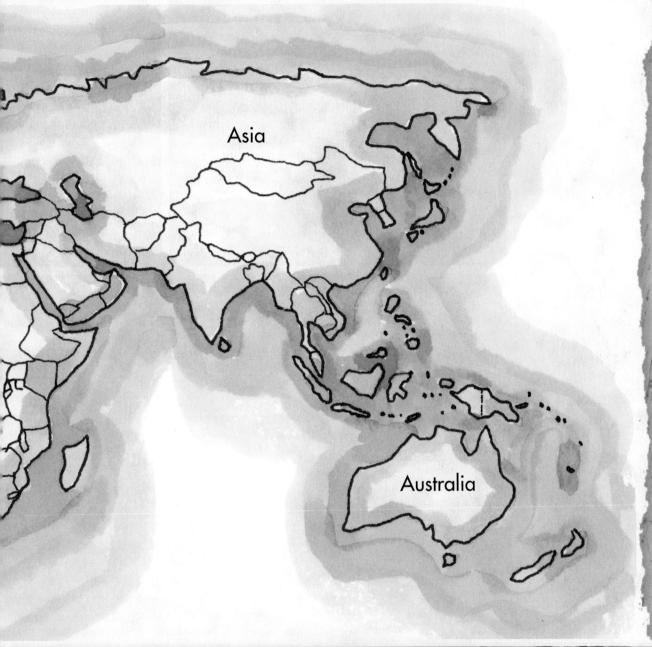

Asia

Australia

Immigrants arrive in the United States from hundreds of countries. In the early 1900s most immigrants came from Europe. Later people came from Asia, Latin America, and Africa.

Why does someone leave the place where he or she was born? Some immigrants left their homes to have freedom. Some left to escape wars. Some left to find jobs. But almost all left to find a better way of life.

Many immigrants arrive in this country with very little. Instead, they bring with them a way of life, including their foods, their celebrations of important events, and their languages. Does your family observe any ethnic celebrations?

4 for you 2 Do

Word Play

Answer the riddle below. Then use this week's concept vocabulary words, or other words you know, to make up your own riddles.

What kind of knee goes on a really long trip?

Making Connections

What new things did the tenement families and Kim Li's family have to face when they came to America?

On Paper

Explain how you could help a newcomer to your school.

Possible answer for Word Play: a journey

82

Let's Eat!

Contents

Let's Eat!

Let's Explore

Words 2 the Wise

Let's eat! We enjoy foods from many different countries. Think about what you like to eat as you read this week's selections.

Let's Explore

Ethnic Foods

It's dinnertime around the world! People are eating different kinds of food. Sometimes we try foods from other lands. We call them ethnic foods. *Ethnic* comes from a Greek word that means "nation."

Long ago there were no trucks. There were no freezers either. People had to eat what they could grow or hunt. They had to plant crops. People planted fruit. They planted grains. And they planted vegetables. Sometimes people sold what they grew.

In Greece the soil is perfect for growing olive trees. Greek people make olive oil with olives. They use olives in many dishes. Try a cold Greek salad with black olives!

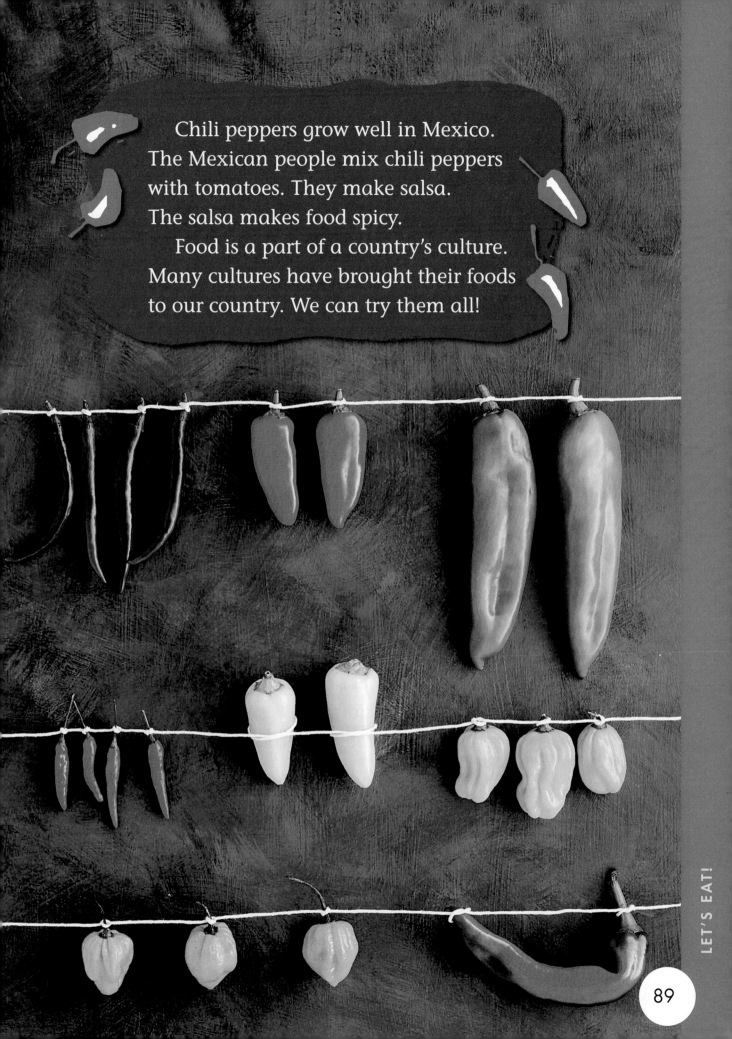

Chili peppers grow well in Mexico. The Mexican people mix chili peppers with tomatoes. They make salsa. The salsa makes food spicy.

Food is a part of a country's culture. Many cultures have brought their foods to our country. We can try them all!

THE FOOD SLEUTH

by Stuart Smith

Did you ever wonder where your favorite food came from? Stu the Food Sleuth is on the case. He will travel to six places to learn about food history!

THE HAMBURGER

Germany

Hi—Stu the Food Sleuth here, and I'm on the case! Let's travel to six places where delicious foods started.

People in Hamburg, Germany, say that they were the first to cook chopped beef. That was about seven hundred years ago.

They started with chopped up beef. Then they added a mixture of spices. Finally they cooked the beef. They called it Hamburg steak.

Today we eat hamburgers on a bun. Hamburgers were first put on bread in the United States. Some say it was first done in Texas. Others say Wisconsin, New York, or Connecticut. At least the bun is all-American!

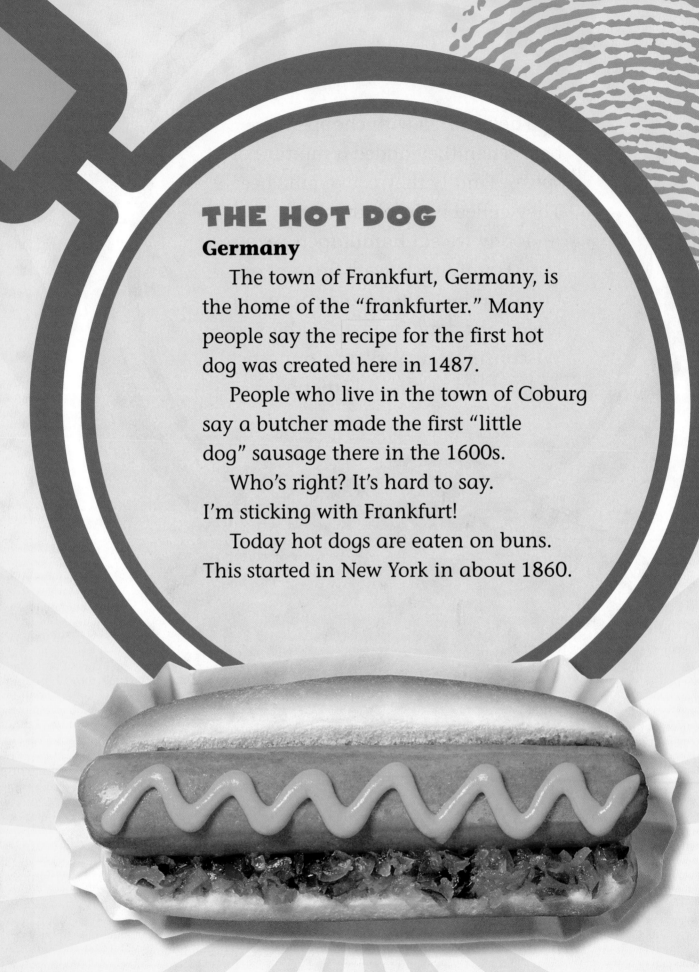

THE HOT DOG

Germany

The town of Frankfurt, Germany, is the home of the "frankfurter." Many people say the recipe for the first hot dog was created here in 1487.

People who live in the town of Coburg say a butcher made the first "little dog" sausage there in the 1600s.

Who's right? It's hard to say. I'm sticking with Frankfurt!

Today hot dogs are eaten on buns. This started in New York in about 1860.

POTATOES

Peru

Long ago, explorers from Spain were looking for gold in Peru. They found gold. They also found potatoes. The explorers took potatoes back to Spain.

Potatoes quickly spread to England, Ireland, and France. They came to America in the 1600s.

How do you like your potatoes? Mashed, baked, or fried? Maybe potatoes are better than gold. They are one of the four most common foods in the world.

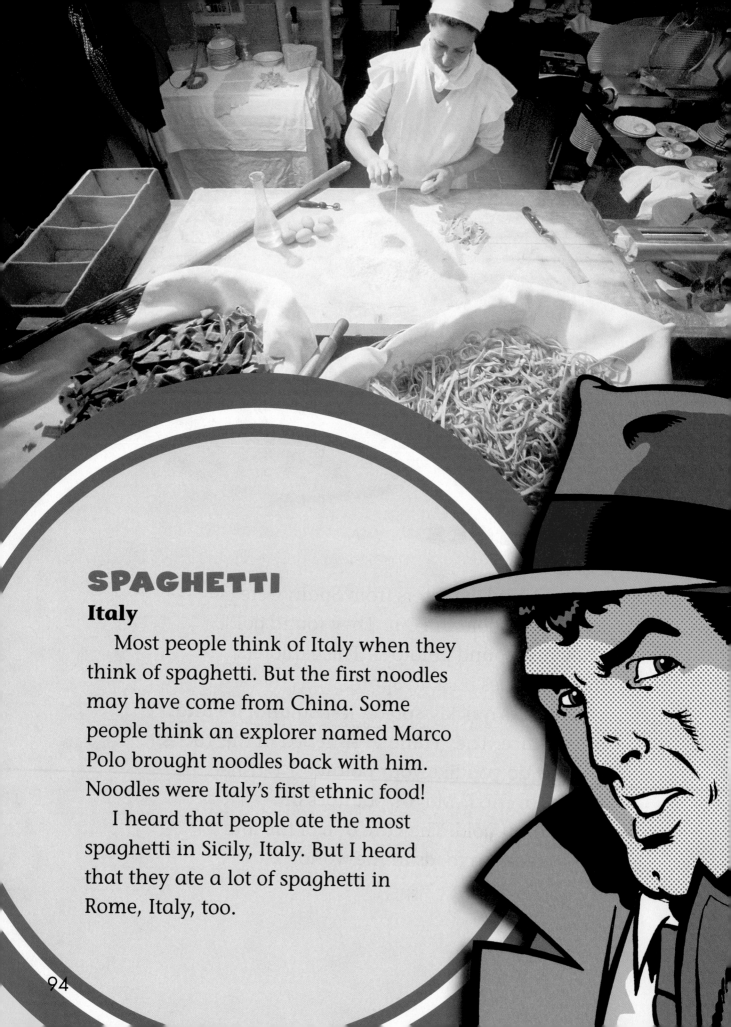

SPAGHETTI

Italy

Most people think of Italy when they think of spaghetti. But the first noodles may have come from China. Some people think an explorer named Marco Polo brought noodles back with him. Noodles were Italy's first ethnic food!

I heard that people ate the most spaghetti in Sicily, Italy. But I heard that they ate a lot of spaghetti in Rome, Italy, too.

Today people like all kinds of noodles. People call it pasta. They like thin noodles. They like wide noodles. They like pasta that looks like tubes. They even like pasta that looks like bow ties!

At dinnertime in America, we often eat spaghetti with meatballs. This was first eaten in Naples. That's in Italy too!

TACOS

Mexico

Tortillas are a type of bread that is round and very flat. They are used to make tacos. People have eaten tacos for a long time. The first ones were made from corn. They were soft, not hard.

Tacos can be stuffed with any filling. Some of the first tacos were filled with fish. Scientists learned that ancient Mexicans also ate insects in tacos.

I like mine with beef and beans!

APPLE PIE

Colonial America? No—England!

Some people think apple pie is an American food. But it may not be American!

So where were delicious apple pies first made? It probably happened in England. A recipe from 1545 was found in England. It was for a pie with green apples. It might be the first apple pie recipe.

Time to sign off now! Remember, good foods have good stories to go with them. Keep looking for them.

WHAT DO YOU THINK?

Are hot dogs and apple pie all-American foods? Why or why not?

STU

The Sweet Surprise

by Katee Davis

illustrated by Laura Ovresat

Ling was a new student at Sands School. Ling had lived in three places before. She had lived in Ohio, Baltimore, and Taiwan.

The kids in her new class were curious. "Will you find a costume for our parade this fall? Will you help with the garden project?"

"I'll try," Ling replied.

Gina, Bill, and Jon sat with Ling at lunch. "Do you want to trade?" Ling asked. The others waited.

Ling took out a shiny piece of white fruit. She took out a crabcake. Then she took out a tamale. Last she took out two wooden sticks called chopsticks.

Bill said, "Tamales! I have had those! Do you want some of my cold pizza? It is from a restaurant near my house."

"OK. I'll try it," said Ling.

Jon said, "Do you want half of my peanut butter sandwich? I'll try that round thing."

Ling took the sandwich. Then she gave him half of the crabcake. "I used to eat these in Baltimore," she said.

Gina looked at the white fruit. Ling picked up the fruit with the chopsticks. "Do you want to try this?" asked Ling.

"What is it like?" Gina asked.

"It tastes sweet," said Ling.

Gina had honey cookies. "My grandpa Jacob keeps bees. We get the honey and make cookies!" said Gina.

Gina looked at the fruit. Then she looked at the cookies. "OK. I'll try the fruit. What is it?"

"It is a litchi (LEE chee) nut," Ling said. Gina bit a tiny piece. The others watched.

"It's good!" Gina said. "It doesn't taste like a nut. I'll call it a yum-yum!"

Ling invited the kids to her house for dinner.

At Ling's house, they went into the kitchen. Ling's mother was cooking. "Ling told me that you tried new foods at lunch," she said. "Would you like to try to cook too?"

She put food in a wide round pan called a wok. She helped the kids put little stuffed pies into the pan. They watched them turn golden brown. The pies smelled delicious.

"Mmm—pot stickers," said Ling. "You'll love them."

"Gina, you can start the egg drop soup," said Ling's mother. They heated chicken broth. Gina dropped in an egg. She stirred it very fast.

Ling's mom helped Jon put pea pods, bean sprouts, and beef in the wok. Jon stirred the mixture.

Ling's mom helped Jon pour the food from the wok on top of cooked noodles. Ling told everyone that it was lo mein (LO mayn).

Ling set the table. Her father sat down. He used his chopsticks. Jon and Bill tried theirs.

Gina said, "I can't hold these. I tried at a restaurant once."

After dinner they had dessert. "Have some rice balls."

Gina was ready to try something new. "Yum-yum," she said.

"That gives me an idea," said Ling. She got a litchi. She opened a rice ball. "I put in a yum-yum. Now it has a surprise inside."

"Why don't you take some to school?" Gina said. "Everybody would love to try them."

After dessert Ling's mom helped the kids make many litchi rice balls.

The next day they served the treats at school. Everybody said, "Yum-yum!"

What Do YOU Think?

What is Ling like?
How do you know?

Menu, Please!

You can make a tasty meal with these easy recipes. This food will take you around the globe!

Main Course .Mexican Cheesy Chili

This meat and bean dish is cooked just right. Watch out—the sauce is spicy!

1 pound hamburger meat
1 can kidney beans
1 can chopped tomatoes
1 tablespoon chili spice
½ pound cheese

1. Cook the meat and drain the oil.
2. Add the beans and tomatoes to the meat.
3. Stir in the spice.
4. Cook for 1 hour on low.
5. Shred the cheese. Sprinkle it on top. Enjoy!

Dessert  Rice Pudding from India

**This sweet treat is called payasam (PAH yuh sum).
Eat it hot or cold.**

5 cups milk

¾ cup condensed milk

¼ cup sugar

1 cup rice

¼ cup cashew nuts

¼ teaspoon ground cardamom

1. Mix the milk, condensed milk, sugar, and rice in a medium-sized saucepan.
2. Cook over medium heat and stir.
3. When the mixture boils, set the heat at low.
4. Cover the pan and cook for about 45 minutes.
5. When the rice mixture is very thick, take the pan from the heat. The rice should be tender.
6. Stir in cardamom and cashews. Serve it warm or cold.

4 you 2 Do

Word Play

How many words can you think of that mean *delicious*? With a partner, list at least four words that describe how good something tastes. If you get stuck, think about your favorite food!

Making Connections

How are some of Ling's Chinese foods similar to some of the foods Stu the Food Sleuth found?

On Paper

Congratulations! You just opened your own restaurant. You want to serve food from all over the world. What three ethnic dishes would you offer? Write clever names for them and describe each dish.

Contents

OTHER TIMES, OTHER PLACES

Let's Explore

Words 2 the Wise

Living in a new place can be exciting. Think about **other times and other places** that you know about as you read this week's selections.

Changing Places

Have you heard tales of great adventure? In an instant you can be part of one.

You don't have to travel to faraway places. Discover other times and other places in books. Stories about King Arthur can transport you to a time long ago.

Experience great adventures in books.

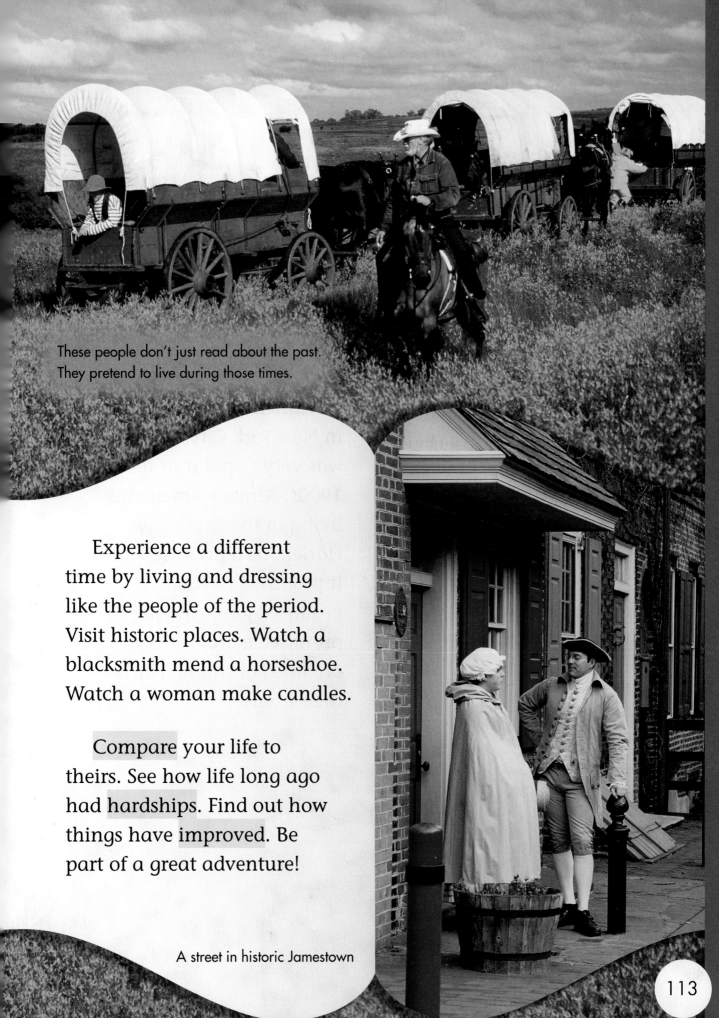

These people don't just read about the past. They pretend to live during those times.

Experience a different time by living and dressing like the people of the period. Visit historic places. Watch a blacksmith mend a horseshoe. Watch a woman make candles.

Compare your life to theirs. See how life long ago had hardships. Find out how things have improved. Be part of a great adventure!

A street in historic Jamestown

113

HOME TO HARLEM

Harlem is a neighborhood in New York City. Harlem was very popular in the early 1900s. African Americans living in the South saw Harlem as a promised land. It promised freedom. It promised jobs. And it promised culture. They dreamed of calling Harlem their home.

African Americans faced many hardships in the South after the Civil War. Laws separated black people and white people. African Americans had to go to different schools. They had to go to different hospitals. They had to eat in different restaurants. They were not allowed to vote.

African Americans wanted to improve their lives. They wanted to leave these hardships behind. Many looked to the North. The North was a place of hope.

Many Harlem restaurants served Southern foods.

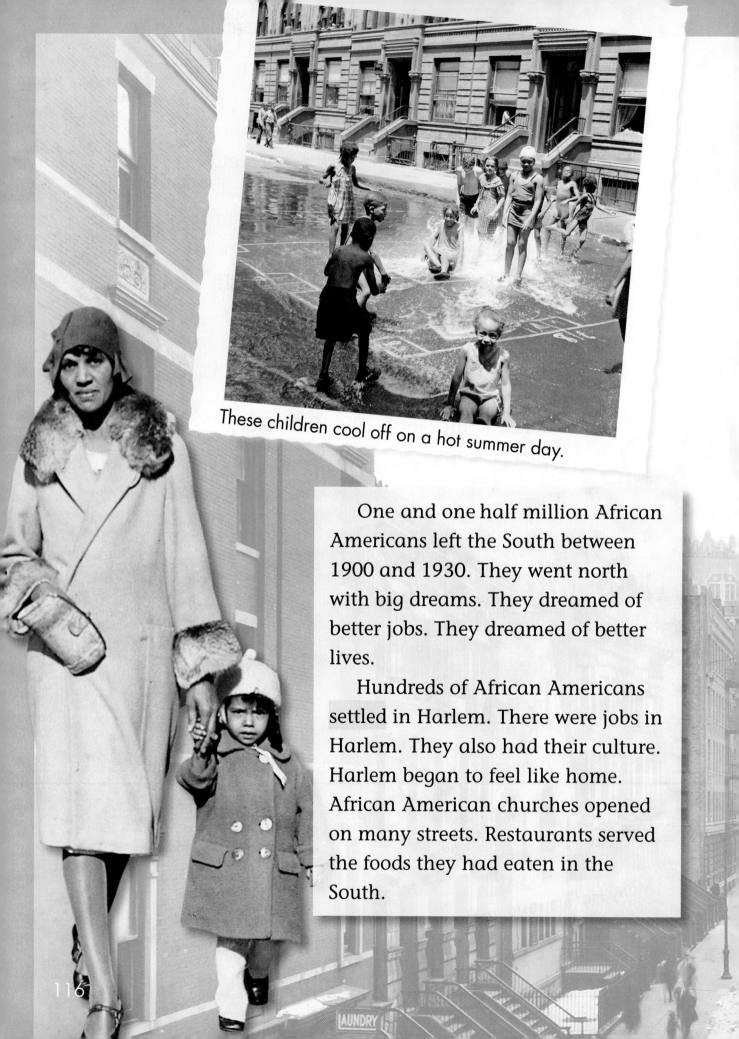

These children cool off on a hot summer day.

One and one half million African Americans left the South between 1900 and 1930. They went north with big dreams. They dreamed of better jobs. They dreamed of better lives.

Hundreds of African Americans settled in Harlem. There were jobs in Harlem. They also had their culture. Harlem began to feel like home. African American churches opened on many streets. Restaurants served the foods they had eaten in the South.

In Harlem, African Americans were police officers. They ran newspapers. They owned stores. Most of these jobs did not make African Americans rich. Still, some black people did make money in Harlem.

Reporters type and edit in a Harlem newsroom.

African Americans owned stores and other businesses.

Lillian Harris settled in Harlem. She started a business. She filled a baby stroller with pig's feet and other Southern foods. Her new neighbors were homesick for Southern cooking. They were happy to buy Lillian's food. People began to call Lillian "Pig Foot Mary." Her business grew through hard work. Pig Foot Mary saved enough money to buy some buildings. She became a rich person.

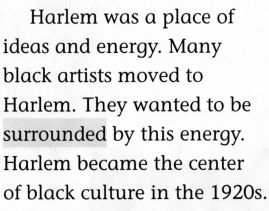

Harlem was a place of ideas and energy. Many black artists moved to Harlem. They wanted to be surrounded by this energy. Harlem became the center of black culture in the 1920s.

Many African American writers lived in Harlem. One writer was Langston Hughes. Langston Hughes was born in Missouri. He dreamed of going to Harlem. "I was in love with Harlem long before I got here," Hughes said.

Langston Hughes

Hughes was also proud of his black culture. He wrote about black people, black music, and black life. He listened to the sounds that surrounded him. Then he turned it all into poetry.

Duke Ellington also moved to Harlem. He was a musician. He and his band played Harlem's most popular clubs. Duke Ellington's music became famous all over the world.

Duke Ellington

Life in Harlem was not perfect. Many African Americans worked very hard to improve their lives. Still, most black people who moved to Harlem stayed there. They let their spirit shine in writing, music, and art. Harlem was in the North, but it was a place of their own. Harlem became home.

WHAT DO YOU THINK?

What made Harlem feel like home for many African Americans?

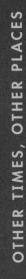

A Trip Back in Time

by James G. Goller

During colonial times, Williamsburg was the capital of Virginia. Williamsburg had many shops. Travelers enjoyed the fine places to stay in the town. In those days, small hotels served food and drinks. There were taverns or public houses. People in town used the taverns as meeting places.

People came from all over to visit Williamsburg. It was a busy and important town.

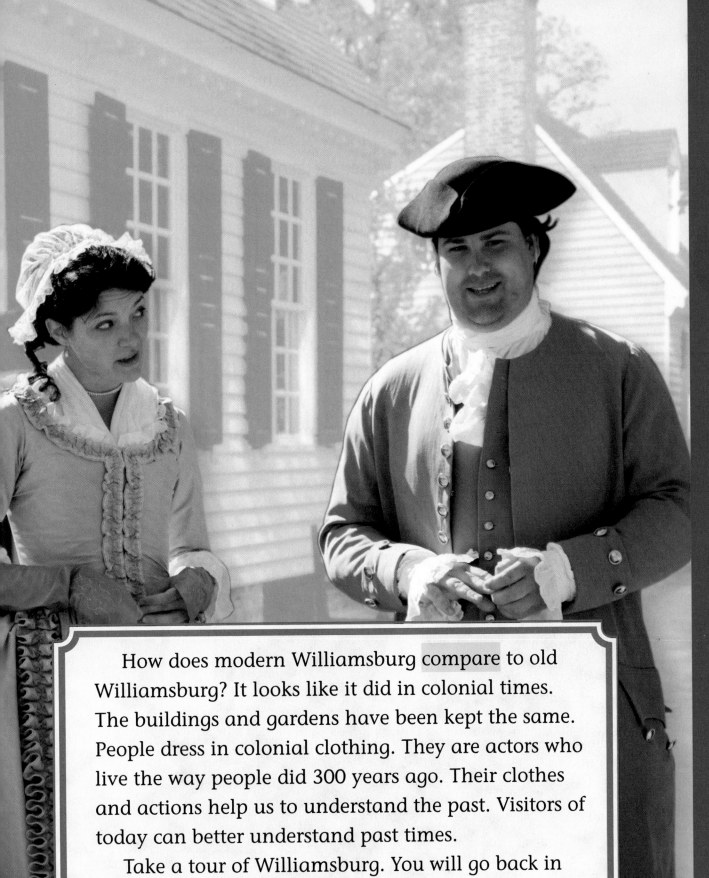

How does modern Williamsburg compare to old Williamsburg? It looks like it did in colonial times. The buildings and gardens have been kept the same. People dress in colonial clothing. They are actors who live the way people did 300 years ago. Their clothes and actions help us to understand the past. Visitors of today can better understand past times.

Take a tour of Williamsburg. You will go back in time 300 years.

You'll start your tour in a carriage. Horses will pull it along. You'll pass the Governor's Palace. You might catch a glimpse of the windmill.

Your driver will turn down the main street in town. It is filled with shops.

Today, this street is clean and smooth. During colonial times it was just the opposite. It was muddy and bumpy!

This person checks a page fresh from the printing press.

First stop is the printing shop. Here you can watch a printer make a newspaper. The worker uses an 18th century printing press. The newspaper is printed one page at a time. The words for a page must be set letter by letter. The letters are put in a wooden case. The printer made books too.

Blacksmiths in Williamsburg still make items using a hammer and anvil.

It's time to stroll down the street. Pass by the blacksmith's shop. Inside you can see a blacksmith pound iron into tools. Farmers needed tools. Workers in other trades needed tools too. They could go to the blacksmith in Williamsburg.

Colonists were interested in fashion and style. Look in the hatmaker's window. It shows the latest colonial style of hats and fans.

Colonial women stopped at the hatmaker's shop to see the newest styles in hats, fans, and gloves.

Wigs were very popular in colonial times.

Let's visit the wigmaker's shop across the street. Inside, the shopkeeper greets you. She explains the different styles of wigs. She also shows you how they were made.

Wigs were very stylish then. They were expensive. Only the wealthy colonists could afford wigs. Men who wore wigs had to shave their heads every day!

More than half the people living in Williamsburg during colonial times were African American slaves.

Next door is Wetherburn's Tavern. Go around to the back. You will see a smaller building there. An African American colonist will greet you. This is her home. She compares the life of white colonists to the life of slaves. The slaves lived behind the fine homes. Some cooked and cleaned for the white colonists. Others worked in the shops.

What Do You Think?

Why do people of today live as colonists used to in Williamsburg?

129

Living as the Colonists Did

Williamsburg, Virginia

Do you want to travel back in time? Take a trip to Williamsburg, Virginia. Williamsburg is a town where you can learn about the past. Here people live and work as the settlers did. They live like colonists in America during the 1700s.

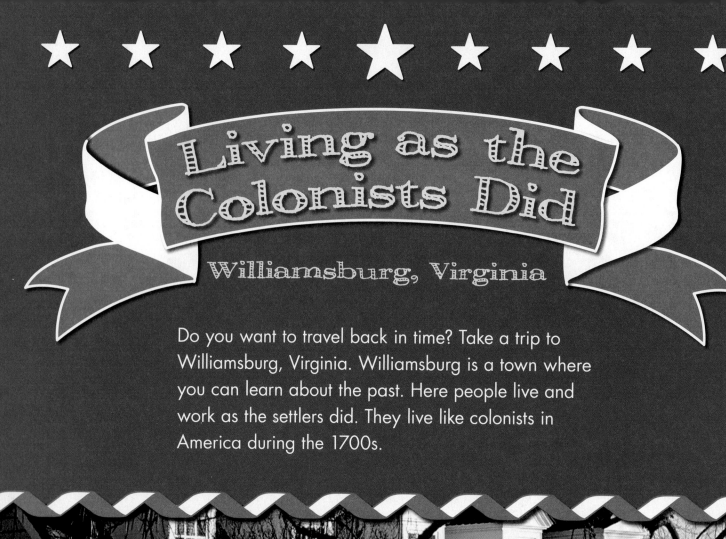

How would you get around?

You would not have a car. Only horse-drawn carriages are allowed on the streets!

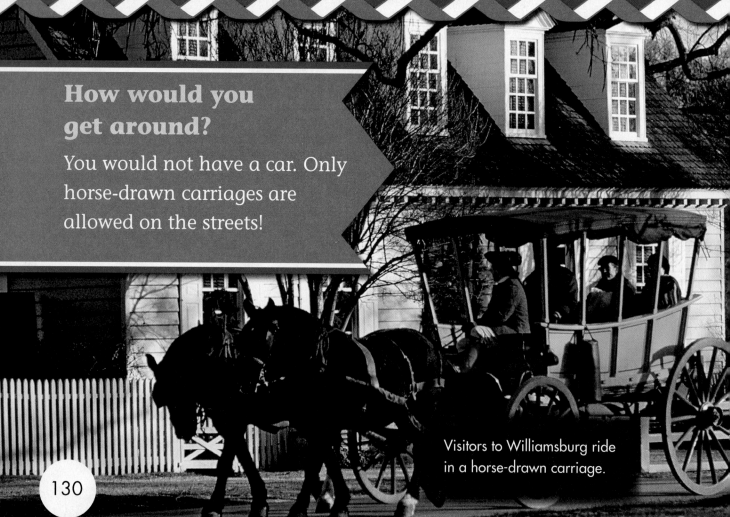

Visitors to Williamsburg ride in a horse-drawn carriage.

What would you do for fun?

Colonial children had many chores. But they did have some free time. Skittles was a favorite game. It was similar to bowling.

Bowling came from the colonial game Skittles.

131

Where would you buy your clothes?

Most colonists did not buy their clothes. They made them. They made cloth from sheep's wool and a plant called flax.

Girls learned to sew at a very young age.

What job would you have?

There were many different jobs in Williamsburg. Wigmakers, woodworkers, barrelmakers, shoemakers, and basketmakers were just a few of the jobs you might have.

Making barrels was an important job in Colonial Williamsburg.

132

Where would you go if you were sick?

There weren't many doctors. Instead, you would visit the apothecary (uh-POTH-i-kair-ee). The apothecary made medicine from plants, roots, and bark.

The apothecary ran the local drugstore.

Colonists came to America to improve their lives. For some, the hardships in America were too great. Others were successful. Imagine that you are living like a colonist for one day. Would you think of it as a great adventure?

4 YOU 2 DO

Word Play

Change these words into their opposites. Use the dictionary or glossary for help.

improve   opposite
settle   hardship

Making Connections

You've read about how people lived in the past. Would you like to live in the past? Explain why or why not.

On Paper

Have you ever visited a new place? Write about how you felt.

Possible answers for Word Play: improve/fail, opposite/same, settle/move, hardship/easy thing

Glossary

ad·dress (ad´ res), *NOUN.* the place to which mail is sent: *She wrote the address on the postcard.* *PL.* **ad·dress·es.**

a·part·ment (ə pärt´ mənt), *NOUN.* a room or group of rooms to live in: *Our apartment is in the same building as my cousin's.*

cloth·ing (klō´ ᴛHing), *NOUN.* coverings for the body: *This store sells men's clothing.*

com·pare (kəm pâr´), *VERB.* to find out or point out how people or things are the same and how they are different: *We can compare the characters from the two books.* **com·pared, com·par·ing.**

136

coun·try (kun´ trē), NOUN.

1. a land where a group of people live under the same government: *England is a country in Europe.*
2. the land where someone was born or where he or she is a citizen: *The United States is my country.*

PL. **coun·tries.**

cul·ture (kul´ chər), NOUN. the beliefs, arts, and tools of a country or people: *People shake hands to greet each other in American culture.*

cus·tom (kus´ təm), NOUN. an old or popular way of doing things: *It was the custom at that time for girls to wear dresses everyday.*

dec·ade (dek´ ād), NOUN. a period of ten years: *From 2001 to 2011 is a decade.*

a in hat	ō in open	sh in she
ā in age	ȯ in all	th in thin
â in care	ô in order	ᴛʜ in then
ä in far	oi in oil	zh in measure
e in let	ou in out	⌐ a in about
ē in equal	u in cup	e in taken
ėr in term	u̇ in put	ə = i in pencil
i in it	ü in rule	o in lemon
ī in ice	ch in child	⌐ u in circus
o in hot	ng in long	

de·li·cious (di lish′ əs), ADJECTIVE. very good-tasting: *We ate a delicious cake.*

din·ner·time (din′ ər tīm), NOUN. when you eat the main meal of the day: *In our house dinnertime is at 6:00 P.M.*

eth·nic (eth′ nik), ADJECTIVE. related to a group of people from the same race, nationality, or culture: *We shared different foods at the ethnic festival.*

hard·ship (härd′ ship), NOUN. a very difficult experience: *The loss of a job can be a hardship for a family.*

im·mi·grant (im´ ə grənt), NOUN. a person who comes into a country to live there: *The new girl in the class was an immigrant from Poland.*

im·prove (im prüv´), VERB. make or become better: *He worked hard to improve his football skills.* **im·proved, im·proving.**

jour·ney (jėr´ nē),
  1. NOUN. a long and sometimes difficult trip: *The family made their journey across the ocean by airplane.*
  2. VERB. to travel; take a trip: *The family journeyed to Australia to vacation.* **jour·neyed, jour·ney·ing.**

lan·guage (lang´ gwij), NOUN. the speech of one nation or other large group of people: *In the United States, English is the language most people use.*

a in hat	ō in open	sh in she
ā in age	ȯ in all	th in thin
â in care	ô in order	ŦH in then
ä in far	oi in oil	zh in measure
e in let	ou in out	⎡ a in about
ē in equal	u in cup	⎢ e in taken
ėr in term	ủ in put	ə = ⎨ i in pencil
i in it	ü in rule	⎢ o in lemon
ī in ice	ch in child	⎣ u in circus
o in hot	ng in long	

mix·ture (miks´ chər), NOUN. a combination of different things: *The meal was a mixture of chicken, rice, and beans.*

mu·se·um (myü zē´ əm), NOUN. a place to display things related to science, art, life in another time or place, or other subjects: *The art museum contained many famous paintings.*

op·po·site (op´ ə zit), ADJECTIVE. as different as can be: *Night is the opposite of day.*

or·di·nar·y (ôrd´ ner´ ē), ADJECTIVE. regular, normal, not special: *I had an ordinary chicken sandwich for lunch.*

pho·to·graph (fō´ tə graf), NOUN. a picture you make with a camera: *She took a photograph of her little brother on his first birthday.*

pop·u·lar (pop´ yə lər), ADJECTIVE. liked by most people: *The roller coaster is a popular ride at the park.*

rec·i·pe (res′ ə pē), *NOUN.* the steps to follow to make a kind of food: *Her mom gave her a recipe for the brownies.*

res·taur·ant (res′ tə ränt or res′ tər ənt), *NOUN.* a place to buy and eat a meal: *We had dinner at a restaurant on my birthday.*

set·tle (set′ l), *VERB.* to go to live in a new place: *The family will settle near their cousins in New York.* **set·tled, set·tling.**

sim·i·lar (sim′ ə lər), *ADJECTIVE.* alike in some way: *The two sisters look very similar.*

a in hat	ō in open	sh in she
ā in age	ȯ in all	th in thin
â in care	ô in order	ᴛʜ in then
ä in far	oi in oil	zh in measure
e in let	ou in out	┌ a in about
ē in equal	u in cup	│ e in taken
ėr in term	u̇ in put	ə = ┤ i in pencil
i in it	ü in rule	│ o in lemon
ī in ice	ch in child	└ u in circus
o in hot	ng in long	

style (stīl), *NOUN.* the current custom in dress; fashion: *She wore dresses in the latest style.*

sur·round (sə round´), *VERB.* to shut something in on all sides: *The water surrounds the island.* **sur·round·ed, sur·round·ing.**

tra·di·tion (trə dish´ ən), *NOUN.* a custom or belief that you learned from your grandparents and parents: *Making cupcakes is a birthday tradition in my family.*

trans·fer (tran sfėr´ or tran´ sfėr),
1. *NOUN.* a change in job or school location: *She will go to another school because of her father's job transfer.*
2. *VERB.* to change or move from one person or place to another: *The nurse was transferred to another department.* **trans·ferred, trans·fer·ring.**

142

Acknowledgments

Illustrations

Cover: Laura Ovresat; **2, 32, 52** Jim Steck; **6, 20–26, 138** David Sheldon; **33, 44–50** Gary Phillips; **58, 70–77, 139** Martha Aviles; **98–104** Laura Ovresat.

Photographs

Every effort has been made to secure permission and provide appropriate credit for photographic material. The publisher deeply regrets any omission and pledges to correct errors called to its attention in subsequent editions.

Unless otherwise acknowledged, all photographs are the property of Pearson Education, Inc.

Photo locators denoted as follows: Top (T), Center (C), Bottom (B), Left (L), Right (R), Background (Bkgd)

Cover: (CR) Buddy Mays/Corbis, (CR) Getty Images, (CL) Paul Chesley/Getty Images; **3** (C) Brian Hagiwara/Jupiter Images, (T) Poodles Rock/Corbis, (BR) Richard Nowitz/Corbis; **5** (C) Donna Day/Getty Images; **6** (B) Getty Images; **7** (C) Peter Dazeley/Getty Images; **8** Ken Chernus/Getty Images; **9** (C) Getty Images; **10** (BL) Getty Images, (BR) Michael Melford/Getty Images, (T) Peter Dazeley/Getty Images; **11** (T) Jim Cummins/Getty Images, (BL) Peter Dazeley/Getty Images; **12** (C) Thislife Pictures/Alamy Images; **13** (TL, BL) Getty Images, (TL) Hulton Archive/Getty Images, (BL) Wides & Holl/Getty Images; **14** (TL) George Marks/Getty Images, (CR) General Photographic Agency/Getty Images; **15** (TL) ©Royalty-Free/Corbis, (BR) Brand X Pictures, (TL) Getty Images; **17** (CL) Getty Images; **18** (BC) G. Schuster/Corbis, (BC) Getty Images; **19** (C) ©Royalty-Free/Corbis, (BR) Getty Images, (C) Hulton Archive/Getty Images, (L) Olivier Ribardiere/Getty Images; **28** (BL) Getty Images, (L) Hulton Archive/Getty Images, (BR) Robin Lynne Gibson/Getty Images; **29** (BC) Bailey-Cooper Photography/Alamy Images, (R) Dex Image/Getty Images, (TL) Getty Images, (BR) Pictorial Press/Alamy Images; **31** (C) ©Daniel Pangbourne Media/Getty Images; **34** (T) Paul Seheult/Corbis; **35** (T) Anders Ryman/Corbis, (B) Witold Skrypczak/Getty Images; **36** (B) Coneyl Jay/Getty Images; **37** (TR) Elsa/Getty Images, (B) Philip J Brittan/Getty Images; **38** (TR) Creatas , (TL) Getty Images, (B) ©Yoshikazu Tsuno/AFP/Newscom; **39** (BR) ©Royalty-Free/Corbis, (TR) Peter Dazeley/Corbis; **40** (TL) Getty Images, (TL) steven mark/Jupiter Images; **41** (C) Kazuhiro Nogi/Staff/Getty Images; **42** (TL) Jeremy Hoare/Alamy Images; **43** (B) Ulrike Preuss/Alamy Images; **53** (BR) ©Royalty-Free/Corbis, (CR) BananaStock, (TL) Design Pics; **54** (B) ©Greatstock Photographic Library/Alamy, (TL) ©Royalty-Free/Corbis; **55** (TL) Lindsay Hebberd/Corbis, (CR) Randy Faris/Corbis; **57** (C) Archive Holdings, Inc./The Image Bank/Getty Images, (Inset) Getty Images; **58** (BC) Ramin Talaie/Corbis; **60** (CC) Image Source/Getty Images; **61** (R) DAJ/Getty Images; **62** (C) Getty Images, (CR) Underwood/Corbis; **64** (TC) Kevin Fleming/Corbis; **65** (BC) Ramin Talaie/Corbis; **66** Getty Images, (BC) Ramin Talaie/Corbis; **67** (TC) Ramin Talaie/Corbis; **68** (CR) Poodles Rock/Corbis; **78** (BL) ©Steve Hamblin/Alamy, (TL) Joe Sohm/Alamy Images; **79** (BR) ©Steve Hamblin/Alamy; **80** (TC) ©Clark Brennan/Alamy, (CR) ©Dinodia Images/Alamy, (C) ©Shotfile/Alamy, (TL) Bettmann/Corbis, (BL) Tony Freeman/PhotoEdit; **81** (BR) ©David R. Frazier Photolibrary, Inc./Alamy, (TR) DAJ/Getty Images, (TL, CR) Omni Photo Communications; **83** (C) Britt Erlanson/Getty Images; **84** (BR) Brian Hagiwara/Jupiter Images; **85** (L) Bob Elsdale/Getty Images; **86** (CL) Bob Elsdale/Getty Images; **87** (TC) Phil Schofield/Getty Images; **88** (C) Ian O'Leary/Getty Images; **89** (C) Amanda Heywood/Getty Images; **90** (T) John Richardson/Getty Images; **91** (BC) Brand X Pictures; **92** (BC) Brand X Pictures; **93** (T) Getty Images; **94** (BR) Getty Images, (T) Owen Franken/Corbis; **95** (TC) Jupiter Images; **96** (C) Brian Hagiwara/Jupiter Images; **97** (BR) John Richardson/Getty Images; **107** (CL) Richard Jung/Jupiter Images, (TR) Rick Souders/Jupiter Images; **108** (BL) Jupiter Images; **109** (B) ©Royalty-Free/Corbis, (T) Lake county museum/Corbis; **110** (CR) ©Photo Collection Alexander Alland, Sr./Corbis; **112** (L) Edmund Blair/Getty Images, (C) Siri Stafford/Getty Images; **113** (T) ©Dave G. Houser/Corbis, (BR) Richard Nowitz/Corbis; **114** (BL) Lucien Aigner/Corbis, (Bkgd) Underwood & Underwood/Corbis; **115** (BC) Lucien Aigner/Corbis; **116** (T) ©Photo Collection Alexander Alland, Sr./Corbis, (CL, Bkgd) Underwood & Underwood/Corbis; **117** (C) Lucien Aigner/Corbis; **118** (TC) Lucien Aigner/Corbis, (Inset) Underwood & Underwood/Corbis; **119** (BR) Corbis; **120** (R) Bettmann/Corbis, (Bkgd) Underwood & Underwood/Corbis; **122** (Bkgd) Buddy Mays/Corbis; **123** ©Irene Abdou/Alamy; **124** (TL, Bkgd) Tim Wright/Corbis; **125** (Bkgd) Andre Jenny/Alamy Images, (TL) Colonial Williamsburg Foundation; **126** (TC, Bkgd) Colonial Williamsburg Foundation; **127** (TL) Buddy Mays/Corbis, (CL) Colonial Williamsburg Foundation; **128** (TC) Tim Wright/Corbis, (B) ©Jeff Greenberg/Alamy; **129** (TL) Buddy Mays/Corbis, (R, Bkgd) Richard Nowitz/Corbis; **130** (B) Richard Nowitz/Corbis; **131** (C) Richard Nowitz/Corbis; **132** (B) Dave G. Houser/Corbis, (T) Richard T. Nowitz/Corbis; **133** (C) ©Richard T. Nowitz/Corbis; **136** (C) Ramin Talaie/Corbis; **142** (TR) Getty Images.